Allegic to Stairs
by Matt Gopsill

First published in 2021 by SanRoo Publishing in Leicestershire, UK.
All Rights Reserved.
Copyright© Matt Gopsill 2021

The right of Matt Gopsill to be identified as the author of this work has been asserted by him in accordance with the Copyright, Designs and Patents Act 1988. No portion of this publication should be reproduced without prior permission.

Cover designed by Jerusha Barnett-Cameron
Cover photography by Lesley Gopsill

Proudly published July 2021 in Leicester, UK,
by SanRoo Publishing,
26 Bramble Way, Leicester, LE3 2GY, U.K.
www.sanroopublishing.co.uk

ISBN 978-09957078-8-7

Contents

A Light Blinks..1
A Little Lamb had Mary....................................3
After the Apocalypse.......................................6
Allergic to Stairs...8
Best Mates 10
City Where Nobody Knows Your Name..................12
Dying Thoughts...14
Father and Son..16
Invasion..17
It..19
Journey into Nowhere.....................................22
Lone Hero...25
Memory..27
Midnight Rendezvous.....................................28
My Feet Don't Smell.......................................29
New Trust...31
Nightlife...33
Past Friends...35
Public Enemy Number One..............................37
Real Life...39
Roads..41
Speechless..43
Stephen...45
Summer's End...47
The Arrival...49
The Bandersnear..50
The Eruption..52
The Final Meeting..54
The First Bloom...56
The Harbour...57
The Night It Happened..................................59
The Political Poltergeist.................................62
The Trolls..64

Allegic to Stairs

The Two Trees..66
The Unforgettable Poem................................67
The Valley Walls...68
Unseen Interiors..70
Who Wants to...71

About Matt..73

Matt Gopsill

A Light Blinks

A pin-prick of light pierced the gloom,
An insignificant light-emitting diode,
Silently doing it's one and only function,
In the darkness, the tiny red glass glowed.

Catching the attention of the black room,
Eyes fixed on its staring shine,
Nobody interrupting its awaited moment,
Anticipating the world's decline.

The stale air was filled with combined dread,
Which joined the silent breathing,
Complementing the humming air filter,
The unnoticed freshness it was bequeathing.

The red light illuminated a circular area,
Shining off the control's high tech surface,
Antibacterial, none-stick and self-cleaning metal,
The most advanced tool of the human race.

Inside a buried bunker, the light shone,
Weak rays falling onto a lonely word,
Printed in black bold Times New Roman capitals,
'Warning' - read but never heard.

Kindled fires of fear and bitter regret,
In the souls of the most influential men,
Could they have stopped this light illuminating,
The last on earth to be witnessed then.

This insignificant spot of pure red colour,
Joined by thin wires to the outside world,
Sensations that turned to an electrical spark,
As radioactive particles are being hurled.

Allegic to Stairs

Suddenly the silence reached new heights,
The air circulation fan spluttered and stopped,
There was only the glow from the mini red light,
The heavy dullness and heartache dropped.

The once blue and green planet of varied life,
Comes to an end when nobody thinks,
The last life on earth bathing in the red light,
But then with the word 'Warning', a light blinks.

A Little Lamb had Mary

Mary had a little lamb,
Its fleece was white as snow,
Everywhere that Mary went,
The lamb was sure to go.

But that's not the end of the story,
Some details were left out,
The little lamb's top legal team,
Got him off on reasonable doubt.

The lamb had Mary at his side,
Going everywhere he went,
He trained her to clean every trace of them,
If they had to cause an accident.

Mary was an expert in losing evidence,
At the scene of his crimes,
No hoof prints or wool fibres were left,
Just the natural dirt and grime.

Be it the murder of a rival herd,
Or the collection of a golden fleece,
Poor Mary was always left behind,
To clean up for the police.

Little Lamb was a criminal mastermind,
One of the country's most feared,
Famed for bloody violence and no compassion,
Even murderers hid when he neared.

Mary was the safety net,
On whom he heavily relied.
His fixer, cleaner and right hand man,
All his loose ends she tied.

Allegic to Stairs

But as the time and the maiming went on,
Poor Mary had her doubts,
The life of crime wasn't for her,
She wanted to get out.

But with all she'd seen, and all she'd heard,
Little Lamb wouldn't let poor Mary go,
When she asked him, he replied,
If she left, her future would be a no-show.

A few weeks of collecting wool went by,
Mary's feelings of dread heightened,
But when she was hoovering her last eyeball up,
She suddenly felt enlightened.

Mary was the quiet one in the shadows,
The one everybody ignored,
But this time she had to take action,
She had to take down her crime-lord.

The plan and action had to be perfect,
The job without a hitch,
Mary had to be in and out quickly,
Planting evidence pointing to Titch.

Titch was the biggest and baddest ram,
The muscle-man of the sheep world,
But Mary had strands of his coarse black fleece,
She took the box where it lay curled.

She crept to Little Lambs luxurious stable,
In the night's darkest hour,
Quick as a flash his little head rolled off,
And Mary started to thoroughly scour.

Matt Gopsill

The crime scene was meticulously arranged,
Evidence perfectly planted,
Mary was in Spain the very next day,
But Titch didn't have his bail granted.

Mary Mary, quite contrary.
How does your garden grow,
With silver bells and cockle shells,
And pretty maids all in a row.

After the Apocalypse

It was a Tuesday afternoon,
Sunny, with a slight breeze,
Only the leafy trees were rustling,
Offices shut with lost keys.

Only took a second for the apocalypse,
But its echoes will be heard throughout time,
Poets and scholars writing their versions,
With no care for reason or rhyme.

Everyone has their story of hardship,
Their own tragedies or woe,
To them it's the story of the century,
To others some lines people know.

This poem will put those lives together,
People joined by a single moment,
The globe rocking on its ever turning axis,
This massive, earth-shattering event.

The banker with money at her fingertips -
Now the world has no use for her,
No debts for this expert to manage,
Equal to her debt-ridden customers.

The King of a broken country,
Sits on his shattered throne,
Dressed in the land's finest embroidery,
Worthless power all he'd ever known.

The doctor who works all hours of the day,
Stemming the tide of the rampaging sickness,
With tools that weren't built to cope,
Against a devastating global illness.

Matt Gopsill

The footballer once sold for tens of millions,
Now with skills useful to no man,
Attracting the odd glance here and there,
On equal footing with the lowliest fan.

The soldier with highest honours gained,
Sent to lead the courageous troops,
Overwhelmed by the human suffering on show,
Reduced to giving out cups of soup.

The addict going cold turkey to survive,
Seeing babies crawling on the ceiling,
Laying on his lonely and broken bed,
His body a mess but his mind healing.

All these people, their lives upside-down,
From one moment of utter madness,
Planet Earth, shaken to its molten core,
Millions of lives plunged into sadness.

Allergic to Stairs

Unclimbable man-made mountainsides,
Leading to most public domains,
As old as human civilization,
Still visible in ancient remains.

One small step for some men daily,
Some take two at a time,
Others dance up and down them,
But I'm allergic to the climb.

I can't feel that soft carpet,
Under my bare morning feet,
I can't stupidly slide down rails,
Till the floor and I rudely meet.

The top steps are out of bounds,
A hazardous, no-go zone,
With high danger and the risk of death,
Like a river where rapids flow.

The jagged appearance repels me,
Out of reach like cliff-top rocks,
Up my steps lies a land of wonders,
The staircase laughs and mocks.

But no matter how much I try to,
Or the sheer bravery I call on,
My allergy keeps me off the stairs,
Their flights make me move on.

One step beyond my top level,
A staircase to my glass-ceiling,
The words "drinks on the top floor",
Always have left me reeling.

Matt Gopsill

Antihistamines don't relieve me,
My allergies much too strong,
Only ramps and lifts help me,
But I know there's nothing wrong,

I always go 'round unseen ways,
When ordinary people use stairs,
You can take in some private views,
If you drive around in a wheelchair.

Best Mates

Traveling together wherever they go,
Inseparable throughout the day,
Vital to each other's daily routines,
Winding smoothly in every way.

They weave along through crowds of marvel,
Strangers stopping to stare,
Each of them having their own task,
Each of them have to be there.

This partnership is years in the making,
Creating a telepathic bond,
Every movement each of them takes,
Instantly the other responds.

Journeys to the ends of the earth taken,
Or just down to the shop,
Through mud, leaves or just humanity,
These two just don't stop.

Different streets each stroll along,
Passed tents and castles on their hike,
Different races and cultures go by,
Like scenery blurred from your bike.

Both know the other's skills by heart,
The whole greater than its single parts,
Each day tending to their partner's needs,
Ever present from when their work starts.

Over the bumps of daily life
The pair glide with total ease,
People's warnings fall on deaf ears,
They go unheeded where they please.

Matt Gopsill

Holidays in the baking summer weather,
Skidding on the winter ice,
Trudging through golden autumn leaves,
Walking in spring paradise.

Through the years the bond gets stronger,
Showing through the scrapes,
Growing older through shared experiences,
Slowly they both begin to trapes.

As their companionship starts to end,
Knocks from close shaves show,
Wearing joints creak and cogs whine,
Vital components start to go.

Eventually every special pair finishes,
A new partnership being born,
A new wheelchair gets their one and only,
The old one gets a new dawn.

Allegic to Stairs

City Where Nobody Knows Your Name

Alone in a bustling buzz of a crowd,
Unnoticed by friend or stranger,
Familiar streets of unfamiliar faces,
Not knowing safety or danger.

Like a shoal of feeding fish
Repelled by poisonous coral,
Or a stranger walking into a local pub,
Starting a fight only about morals.

Shopping centres and farmers' markets,
Conversations running wild,
A constant stream of sales and banter,
Data gathered and filed.

Fifty percent sales and another ten,
Always done for mate's rates now,
I don't bring or buy anything in this town,
I don't have the friends or knowhow.

Coffee shops selling personalised drinks,
Signing them in finest cocoa,
Their valued customers names on top,
Using beans from Morocco.

I've never tasted the unique normality,
Never been a valued customer,
Unskilled baristas haven't seen me,
Passing through dry in the summer.

The local friendly banking service,
Raring to make your money grow,
Taking your hard earned wages,
And securing it with a bow.

Matt Gopsill

Locking your vault with passwords,
That are just between you two,
I haven't got those premium bonds,
I'm not on the banks who's-who.

All manner of food is now available,
Hot or cold, fast or slow cooked,
The finest dining change can buy,
Just as long as you've pre-booked.

Your name's the only thing required,
To taste the flavour of the world,
But I only eat scavenged morsels now,
As I lay here, tightly curled.

The city where nobody knows my name,
Has been home for all my life,
Bringing up seventeen tiny fox-cubs -
I play a big part in the wildlife.

Dying Thoughts

The hedge trimmer pierced his precious skin,
Falling on the leafy ground,
Surrounded by the privet twigs,
Greenery and loneliness all around.

His alarmed mind started looking for answers,
To mend his and everyone's woes,
Sending messages to complete a checklist,
"First, I can wiggle my toes".

The checklist was filled in and analysed,
The results were very, very clear,
Life wasn't going to be years as thought,
He was going to die right here.

The feeling wasn't panic or cold fear,
He was a practical, sensible man,
His roast chicken dinner was still cooking,
And he hadn't pressed the extractor fan.

At least the alarm will do its job,
Giving the fire service the burden,
Saves him lying under this trimmed bush,
While fertilizing the garden.

The freight train of thoughts still passed,
His will was wonderfully written,
His family and friends would be just fine,
His daughter will love the kitten.

The company he ran would initially lose,
But his secretary knew his passwords,
Tim, his head-hunted second in command,
Would continue making the fake turds.

Thoughts were whirling round his head -
Who would take over the golf club?
Will he get a trophy named in his honour?
Would he get a plaque in the pub?

Then a more ethereal subject entered,
Where was he going next?
Would heaven be as good as they said?
He had never read the fine text.

Would there be a strict dress code?
He had never looked good in a toga,
What extra activities were provided?
He hoped to God it wasn't yoga.

But what if he went the other way,
He wasn't a big fan of high heat,
What were those seven deadly sins,
Finally his laziness admitted defeat.

Suddenly he felt the icy cold breath,
Death was crawling up his leg,
Shouting out his goodbyes to the earth,
For God's forgiveness he began to beg.

The thought train started to slow down,
The end of the track had been reached,
The last thought of this unfortunate man:
"Oh no, I forgot to put on the. . . . . . ."

Father and Son

Jesus said to God while sitting at a great height,
"The world looks good on this black starry night,
All those children of ours sleeping in their beds,
With dreams of goodness going 'round their heads,
All the animals you meticulously created,
All the fiddly bits I know you kind of hated,
Can I ask you father: where you got your ideas from?
And all those personalised organs would cost a bomb! "
"My dear son, take a look and see,
Everything I created fits so perfectly,
All the creatures I painstakingly planned and made,
Have everything they need to live and never fade."
"But Father, why are many of your creations suffering?
Look down there and see that wildebeest staggering."
"You should know all about that my dear boy,
Everything has to die; their atoms I redeploy."
"But O heavenly Father, are you not the creator?
Surely you don't need something else's matter."
"Son, you should have worked out by now,
You can't create something just by saying 'kapow'."
"But Father can I ask the question all wonder:,
How did you create the universe, without going under?"
"Well, my dear boy, I have been keeping this a secret from you,
Your huge pet rabbit didn't go to a far away zoo."

Invasion

Across hills and grassy fields,
Futuristic giants loom,
Colonizing England's pleasant green land,
Threatening an approaching doom.

Reaching to the sky a hundred feet tall,
Powerful arms outstretched,
Surveying their recently acquired vista,
That generations of artists sketched.

A historic yet ever-changing landscape,
Countless seasons in the making,
Agricultural age-lines across its skin,
Growing golden wheat for baking.

The wind of change is gusting through,
Accelerating natural evolution,
Some plants and animals have fallen behind,
In this very unnatural revolution.

This new army of steely-eyed sentinels,
Punctuating the fragile earth,
Creating energy out of fresh sweet air,
Knowing this resource's worth.

Fresh air has gone out of fashion,
Pollution masks will have to return,
Carbon dioxide and methane surround,
From cars and the rubbish we burn.

The impending doom surrounds us,
Invading everywhere we go,
The streets are paved with dirty stones,
But the giants are shouting "No!"

Allegic to Stairs

We see these imposing wind turbines,
As eyesores on the skyline,
But they should be seen as hopeful beacons,
And a stark warning sign.

Matt Gopsill

It

In the heart of the blackened darkness,
Far from the nearest drop of light,
Inside the huge, cavernous mouth of hell,
Something was born in the dead of night.

It screamed to mark its deadly arrival,
Filling the void with an ancient sound,
With arms like tree-trunks and piercing eyes.
It pounded the mud-soaked ground.

Its mother died in untold agony,
Writhing alone in this pit of despair,
Becoming its first freshly-killed meal,
Nourishing It as it became aware.

The appetite for warm blood spawned,
Feeding its growing muscles,
Fuelling the first unholy growth spurt,
Ready for life's grizzly tussles.

With an unearthly roar it stood,
Stretching out its imposing figure,
Skin burned by the fires of the devil,
Its bulk seeming many times bigger.

Taking its first steps on this earth,
The ground was shaking with fright,
The world hasn't seen his like before,
Even the darkness hated the sight.

It burst from its mother's dark grave,
Into a gnarled and silent forest,
Every instance of life ran for cover,
As the new ultimate force progressed.

Allegic to Stairs

The trees smouldered as it passed,
Its body left a black path,
The knotted and knitted branches
Didn't slow its unrelenting wrath.

The edge of forest shone in beams,
Like hundreds of small searchlights,
It doubled its hellbent pace again,
Until it reached the urbanised sights.

Chaos ensued for the city's people,
Panic spread like a deadly plague,
People ran for their fragile existences,
But their destinations were vague.

It was heading to the tallest tower,
Roads crumbled under its hooves,
Without pause it started climbing,
Forcing the birds to move.

Standing where it could be spotted,
By everyone for miles around,
It made a noise that filled air-waves -
Humanity's original homing sound.

Everyone stopped and gazed silently,
Either live or at TV screens near,
It spoke of the usual world domination,
And it would rule with purest fear.

The skies went as dark as midnight,
Thunder now began to crash,
The air was still; the rain came,
Mizzle first, then started to lash.

Matt Gopsill

Rivers drowned the hoof-marked road,
When it called out one last time,
"Bow down to me, your new overlord,
Call me Glitterbob Ralf Fluffytime!"

A hum grew around the soaked streets,
Then a little chuckle rang out,
It grew into a torrent of happiness,
Glitterbob gave out a pained shout.

It clutched its chest in pure agony,
Letting go of the tower ledge,
It fell a hundred floors and died,
Impaled on a large privet hedge.

The rain stopped; the sun shone,
The people got on with their lives,
The hedge grew to ten feet tall,
And never saw a pruning knife.

Journey into Nowhere

On a narrow-boat of holy smoke,
On the river of the other moons,
Passing by newly-sewn fields of gold,
Growing ripe and juicy doubloons.

The river banks are full of holes,
To give you cash withdrawals,
But the wild fatcats undermined them,
Making nests of wobbling morals.

Slowly hurtling through this odd land,
Taking your brain to a new dimension,
Take notice of the safety advice given,
Don't forget to pay close attention.

Put on your seat belt and braces tight,
The exits are all around your boat,
If you feel too dizzy, look at the horizon,
And please don't feed the goat.

I hope you enjoy your wild ride,
On this amazing journey to nowhere,
Free tea and coffee will be self-served,
It's your kettle and cup, to be fair.

Look at that house on the grassy hill,
It's been painted the purest white,
Inside contains this world's big chief,
He's always twitching for a fight.

Feel that rocking under your chair -
The rich soundwaves of this river,
It's constantly streaming music down
A watery net, ready to deliver.

Matt Gopsill

Fluffy white vapor in the sky,
The modern addiction of today,
Laced with tasty useless necessities,
For the people prepared to pay.

A forest of high-rise concrete trees,
The nesting place of the workers,
Not maintained and overgrown,
Some full of darkness-lurkers.

In the distance, the sea of change,
Growing wider with every voice,
Flooding with pure liquid discontent,
Running like a jogging tortoise

An evil monster threatens this land,
A silent and invisible creature,
Born with a loud burst of dirty energy,
Choking kills are its main feature.

Hold on tight for the next stretch,
This bit of river is home to trolls,
Filling the net with unfiltered rubbish,
Ruining the flow with faked lols.

Notice up there on the tallest tree,
The mating display of the birds,
Huge red lips and inflated chests,
With paps flocking round in herds.

This is almost the end of the journey,
Did anyone remember the goat?
His name's Tax and he's so hungry,
He's everywhere I go on the boat.

Allegic to Stairs

One final view before you all leave,
Do you see that mist in the air,
Smoke from old flames of happiness,
Embers now of 'we don't really care'.

I hope you've enjoyed your mind trip,
Through this land of imagination,
I hope you take away your free gift:
New appreciation of your home-nation.

Matt Gopsill

Lone Hero

On the way to see a lonely old man,
I walk on an ancient cobbled road,
Glass smoothed by hundreds of hard shoes,
A proud country continually erodes.

This man was the saviour of Britain's freedom,
Priceless medals in a dusty draw,
Stained beard guarding a row of plastic teeth,
Hiding a soldier's chiselled jaw.

Memories of a sweetheart on dirty walls,
Wooden TV on a chipboard table up loud,
Only the five undefined channels available,
This veteran lives away from the crowd.

Half-shut curtains hiding the hero within,
A beacon of freedom living in the gloom,
Living on pension rations from his homeland,
Coldly distributed in a government room.

An aging house avoided by all the mod cons,
Heat coming from an eighties fake-fire,
Flickering faux daylight flares out,
Whistling sounds of the kettle making choir.

Memories of victories for England etched,
Against all odds and mounting resistance,
For King and country he achieved many miracles,
Daring deeds that all tipped the balance.

I pass the bomb-cracked mid-terrace house,
With its lucky Chinese refugee door,
Arriving at the house of the lone hero,
Its sliding windows from just after the war.

Allegic to Stairs

I knock the antique knocker, scaring dust,
Hearing the loud groaning just after,
A while later my granddad stands in its place,
Face beaming out and filled with laughter.

Memory

Neurons connect with a spider web of axons,
Trapping experiences and places for later,
Storing stories about your past performances,
Aiding your decisions with recalled data.

Filling the film projector of your cinema,
Selling the seats inside your head,
Memories well-edited, from your angle,
Making sense of the random things said.

Directing your past events with precision,
Award-winning filming plays,
Waking the dead to comfort and console,
Giving support when our mood sways.

A HD streaming service from within,
Instant access without passwords or login,
Gigabytes of content freely available,
You only need a memory-jogging.

That unforgettable holiday in a foreign land,
Or family Christmas draped in snow,
Always on-watch, never pay-to-play,
Nor slowing your bandwidth at peak flow.

The organically-grown database on demand,
Solely for you to use and share,
Entertaining people with remembered deeds,
Just using what's beneath your hair.

Subtle connections link each tale,
A special person or familiar story,
The overarching tapestry called your life,
Keeps the viewer hooked to each memory.

Midnight Rendezvous

In the heavy darkness that surrounds, I sit in anticipated wait,
Stars above me wink while they watch, their light years too late,
Subtle pin holes in the blackness, glitter spilt on death's shawl,
Coolness paws at my heated skin, reminding me of winter's call,
Scanning the night for the movement, perfectly camouflaged,
A feather touch on the midnight air, the ghostly figure miraged,
A meticulously designed hunting machine, stealthily prowling the skies,
Wasting no energy in the search for food - I spot its rounded eyes,
We silently watched out together, connected by our sublime sight,
Time froze on our midnight rendezvous, all other thoughts took flight,
Fleeting minutes passed by, only slowing for an impolite glance,
A shrill call broke the rendezvous' tension, my company took the acceptance,
The round eyes homed in on the source, our connection snapped in two,
My company took flight obediently - his mate really needed that shrew.

Matt Gopsill

My Feet Don't Smell

An eerie silence and everything's still,
The room vanished and fog fell,
All I did was remove my socks,
But I know my feet don't smell.

On a sunny beach with bare feet,
The sea begins to swell,
All I did was go for a paddle,
But I'm sure my feet don't smell.

Walking down a street in flip-flops,
Someone ran in front with a bell,
He was warning people of the odour,
But really my feet don't smell.

I was shopping in Leicester market,
The stall holder gave a hard sell,
Two for one odour-eaters at half price,
But surely my feet don't smell.

I spent the afternoon in the park,
But I heard the park keeper yell,
"Get your feet off the grass!"
I thought my feet didn't smell.

I was having a nice relaxing bath,
Washing myself with a flannel,
It rotted away over my feet,
Tell me my feet don't smell.

I booked a holiday in the Maldives
In a swanky five-star hotel,
Shoes off and the fire-alarm began,
I'm positive my feet don't smell.

Allegic to Stairs

All these experiences on my mind,
My feet are on the loose,
I really must come out and say,
I actually hide cheese in my shoes.

Matt Gopsill

New Trust

Trust me, I'm here for you whatever,
Through anything the world throws,
I know I've known you only a few days,
But I'm here wherever the path goes.

I understand you had a rough break up,
A relationship you've had for years,
I know the memories are still so raw,
You are bound to have some fears.

I don't know you and you're the same,
We'll have to grow together,
I'm learning what makes you comfy,
I'll help you to cut the old tether.

We'll have some great experiences,
Traveling together on many sidetracks,
Up hills and down winding roadsides,
Taking each other the long way back.

I know everything is unnatural now,
Like that awkward first kiss,
But with practice and persistence,
You and I know we can do this.

We'll quickly form a dream team,
Everywhere you take me to,
We'll stand out from the masses,
In all we say and do.

Let my new improved technology,
Help you the best I can,
I'll carry you everywhere you need,
We have your future to plan.

Allegic to Stairs

My wheels will get you anywhere,
My seat will support your back,
I'm your brand new wheelchair,
And we have a world to attack.

Matt Gopsill

Nightlife

Ancient lights decorate the darkness,
Gifts from far flung giants,
Grains of brightness from alien solar systems,
Displayed for tonight's street tenants.

A ceiling of beauty half-hidden by pollution,
Smog alight with moss-tinged gloom,
The atmosphere spiked with poisoned gas,
Hinting of life's impending doom.

The city's nightlife live under this blanket,
Safety and comfort a daydream,
Fear and loathing the popular choice,
And survival the overriding theme.

This isn't the high-life of the big city,
The advertised land of opportunity,
That place shuts when the sun descended,
This is a different community.

The crime and disease-riddled population,
Living in the shadows of the high rise,
Death always strolls among them,
Not bothering with his cloaked disguise.

Booze and drugs fuell the activities
Of those that lived the nightlife,
Dependencies drive their economy wild,
Pushed forward with the point of a knife.

Supply and demand is the foundation,
Of the night-markets booming trade,
'Satisfaction guaranteed' - its famed moto,
A thin veil over goods cheaply made.

Allegic to Stairs

Cocaine cut with crystal cleaning powders,
Whiskies and wines watered down,
Stolen goods packaged like brand new items,
No tax returns going to the crown.

The night customers have no buyer's choice,
No comparison sites to look for deals,
It's a seller's market with no regulations,
Prices fall on their greased wheels.

The growing population of the nightlife,
With unhealthy, unbreakable habits,
Have to self-medicate without any doctors,
Their pupils wider than a rabbit's.

The big city's nightlife will take anyone,
No matter their colour or age,
If someone has a disability or an illness,
Nobody's put in a different cage.

Equality lives in the streets of the night,
Unlike in the sun-light of the day,
They can clearly see the people's problems,
But do nothing that's out of their way.

Past Friends

On a street across the emerald island,
Was a circle of cobblestone,
A strange green light burst from the cracks,
With old musical Irish tones.

An unnoticed jade tornado grew,
Disturbing the stones' long-term bed,
Green plumes of timeless swirling flames
Towered overhead.

Passers-by were unaware of the sight,
The revelry of Dublin was all around,
Temple bars serving Ireland's finest,
Thousands of sorrows were drowned.

They didn't notice the army arriving,
The original defenders of the realm,
A platoon of wary leprechauns came,
Their great leader, Fionn, at the helm.

Fionn was the king of the leprechauns,
He was chosen by defeating the beast,
Now he lead a small group of recruits,
In a strange land he knew the least.

With noise and magic all around,
Fantastic beasts rolling down roads,
Brightly coloured lights hiding the stars,
Plaques and signs written in code.

Crowds of every nation bustled blind,
Intoxicated on Dublin's own craic,
Bumping and barging Fionn's followers,
As they went to the Liffe back to back.

Allegic to Stairs

In their own island of timeless safety,
The ultimate formation to defend,
Parting the waves of ceaseless parties,
Set apart from times with no end.

Arriving on the banks of the old river,
Stagnant and abused water flowed,
The fenced off, concreted riversides,
Caged to make way for man's road.

Big tears welled up in Fionn's eyes,
The green rolling hills had moved
For shining forest of stone structures,
Ireland definitely hadn't improved.

Suddenly the group were attacked,
Another platoon surrounded them,
Strangely dressed in capes and masks,
Speaking odd words out of rhythm.

One huge man approached Fionn.
A fearsome opponent he would be,
He took the leprechaun by the hand,
And shook it most heartily.

The two platoons combined that night,
Took on the many temple bars,
Made merry, painted Dublin green,
Listening to lively Irish guitars.

In the morning with heads complaining,
It was time to leave for the past,
The new platoon of the best of friends,
Parted with great memories amassed.

Matt Gopsill

Public Enemy Number One

Incy Wincy spider went up the water spout,
Down came the rain and washed the spider out,
Out came the sun and dried up all the rain,
Incy Wincy spider went up the water spout again.

But the sun couldn't improve poor Incy's mood,
Because some people are so very nasty and rude,
The water spout belonged to a nice young family,
Who wouldn't hurt a tasty fly and let it in happily.

They didn't hurt wasps or put mouse traps down,
They'd even pick up ants although with a frown.
But spiders were public enemy number one there,
Murders committed daily, none of which were fair.

Incy was lucky and escaped down the water spout,
Unfortunately it started raining when he got out.
He was really upset with the persecution of spiders,
He'd read on the spider Web about a group of hiders.

Nearly all his mates had joined this online group,
He was too busy staying hidden to keep in the loop.
Incy thought of all the good things he had helped with,
Fly and pest control for free - plus the biting was a myth.

Only in extreme circumstances where it was life or death,
He'd only nip you and then run away to catch his breath.
He enjoyed the quiet life which included hanging round,

Allegic to Stairs

Watching tv, snacking on flies and not getting drowned.

Quickly he realised the water spout wasn't a good place,
With the frequently occurring torrent in poor Incy's face.
His mind was made up and he was quickly on the move,
Down the spout and straight away finding the exit groove.

Through the soggy garden as fast as his eight legs could -
He definitely wouldn't be outside as he didn't like mud.
Through the hedge to next door and then he saw it,
An old thatched cottage that would be a perfect fit,

Incy crept inside and saw something that made his day,
Cobwebs with all he could eat and the duster hidden away.
In the corner was an old man watching tv turned up loud,
With a documentary's commentary speaking out so proud,

About letting spiders in your home and the benefits you gained,
Incy Wincy spider climbed up the webs in a chain,
Finding a comfy cobweb with a juicy fly near the TV,
He got stuck into a tasty leg and was as happy as could be.

Real Life

Born with a burden around our necks,
Rule-breaking punished or rewarded,
A maze of amazement ring-roading pitfalls,
Each standout achievement recorded.

Mundane actions lost in the commotion,
People losing the human race,
Struggling to get their unique voices heard,
Tripping over their bespoke silk lace.

Most hacking away on rusty chains,
Holding their personalised anchors,
Slowing down with each hit taken,
Unable to get rid of the clingy cankers.

Targets go past in a blur of disappointment,
Dodging people's careful aims,
Lucky shots and fortunate ricochets in need,
To win these rigged fairground games.

Rules and regulations set in good faith,
Designed to help their followers live,
Turned and twisted by the radical man,
Hoping their imaginary friend will forgive.

Images of the perfect life surround,
Abs of steel and plastic boobs pose,
Living in penthouses with golden gates,
All photoshopped so anything goes.

Some designer drugs giving a totes high,
Illegal except for the prescribed few,
Aging medication losing the battle now,
As superbugs come charging through.

Allegic to Stairs

Law-breakers hide behind the law-makers,
Not caring about their caring attitude,
Common sense left out of the commons work,
Looking for the public's mark of gratitude.

Babies born bald and bound by borders,
Children criticized for not being free,
Adults trapped in a cycle of forced work,
Dying in a place that smells like wee.

Real life is the obligatory uphill struggle,
Filled with the rock falls of pressure,
But stop for a moment and see the view,
Your unique life is one to treasure.

Matt Gopsill

Roads

Whether it's paved with good intentions,
Or topped with the finest gold.
The road you walk or drive down,
Ever winding, destination untold.

Curves like a vibrant rainbow,
Hidden dips never clearly warned
The road to absolutely anywhere,
No signposts or directions adorned.

Nowhere to be found on google maps,
A to Z pages too.
This uncharted but well travelled road,
Belongs only to you.

Experiences and memories surround,
Like old, expensive homes.
An obsessive hoarder's possessions.
Gathered from everywhere we roam.

Many other roads intersect it,
Cross or travel side by side.
Some of the surfaces join smoothly,
But others a bumpier ride.

Whether you walk or drive down it,
It's the choice we have to make.
There's no speed limits on this road,
No chugging tractors for you to overtake.

The lay bys are fraught with danger,
On this road of our unique lives.
Stop too long in a place,
And the boredom police arrive.

Allegic to Stairs

There are no driving lessons,
On this tight highway.
You learn on the way down this route,
Your knowledge - no-one else can say.

Views of triumph and suffering,
Go by on each side.
Vistas of a world full of countries,
Pass on this personal joyride.

The length of road is undetermined,
It travels to its own end.
After which is dusty brown earth,
The journey beyond is unpenned.

Matt Gopsill

Speechless

Speechless like a desert island,
In a sea of sound waves,
Serene isolation in a jibba- jabba storm,
Loneliness amongst rants and raves.

You can call everyone on earth,
Just with a press of a button,
Communicate your dull fleeting ideas,
From Baghdad on via Luton.

We all follow the latest fake news,
From Presidents and chavs the same,
Filling the virtual ocean with soundbites,
All want their five kilobytes of fame.

Conversations buzzing everywhere,
Like wasps bouncing off eared walls,
Rooms bursting with words and gestures,
Every moment punctuated with calls.

Sitting in the centre of this commotion,
Hidden behind electronic speech,
Emotionless, void of human feelings,
My immediate ideas out of reach.

Answering the question before this one,
Always lagging behind the mean-time,
Exclamations circling around like whirlwinds,
Never stopping to admire a rhyme.

Contacts happening faster and further,
Quick words and pixelated pictures,
Are words losing their stated meaning,
Writing their gravestones in scriptures?

Allegic to Stairs

Friendly connection requests from Facebook,
A cheery retweet or two,
Instant messages from the one you love,
An emoji shaped like a poo.

Heart to heart chats in two continents,
With the best friend we'll never meet,
Ones and zeros carrying the thoughts,
Emotions captured as minds compete.

Intimate secrets flying free across oceans,
Perfectly ripe for hacking,
A global highway with tailbacks of voices,
The virtual asphalt cracking.

Sitting in the middle of the data storm,
Raining information on all my senses,
I see the world spinning full speed,
Speechlessly watching the consequences.

Matt Gopsill

Stephen

A determined voice trapped inside,
Escaping through a tiny crack,
Universes evolving new life,
But a solid wall holding it back.

Emerging into this world so slowly,
Like a word stuck on your tongue,
The software is running at full speed,
But the hardware's gone wrong.

Imprisoned thoughts growing aware,
Calling from behind mental bars,
Trying to show their unique meanings,
Aiming for their own stars.

Existing in two different time zones,
Neurons running at light speed,
The outside form trying to keep up,
But the mind would always lead.

Aids supporting his physical needs,
But he outruns them with ease,
The fastest processors left for dust,
His wheels even stopping to wheeze.

Travelling to far off objects in space,
Within his own voyaging mind,
Riding a wave of hawking radiation,
Proving the theories he defined.

Writing about history in brief,
Typing with a single switch,
Producing a world-famous non-fiction,
Feeding full, the knowledge rich.

Allegic to Stairs

An ordinary man with a great gift,
Opening up universal secrets,
Breaking out of his famous exterior,
And living a life without any regrets.

Matt Gopsill

Summer's End

Golden leaves clinging on the trees,
Frosts threatening to return.
Hibernation hoards are gathering together,
Guy Fawkes being built to burn.

The sun is growing tired of the heat,
Long days are turning into nights,
The plants are giving out their nightcap berries,
Fuelling birds for their long haul flights.

Mushrooms are showing their marmite heads,
Beautiful and ugly - encapsulating both,
Erupting from the tiring earth,
Worn out from the summer growth.

Chill winds coming in from the roughening sea,
Over the heads of stampeding white horses,
Moving the once packed, ruined-castle sands,
Mini sandstorms reveal atmospheric forces.

Summer showers evolving into winter storms,
Parched relief turning to sodden hate,
Flooded roads and leaves on the tracks,
Summer seems like a far off date.

Hearty stews and roast dinners made,
Replacing light salad lunches,
Slow-cooked meat aromas fill houses,
Giving everyone the munchies.

Central heating wakes to keep the cold at bay,
Pipes banging in protest,
The dormant radiators stir to life,
After a season of not being noticed.

Allegic to Stairs

Cosy fires soon crackle and flare,
Lighting the evenings with a warm hug,
Pets attracted to the orange glow,
Wanting to spend the winter snug.

The long months of darkness loom ahead,
The scarce heat man-made,
But winter's full of closeness and love,
As the summer heat starts to fade.

The Arrival

They point, they stare.
Questions in the air.
The crowd parts like the red sea.
It's not Moses helping people flee,
An audible murmur, a noticeable hum.
The gathering of people begins to succumb,
The new arrival in this herd of human beings
Turned every head from what they were seeing.
The awful awe and revengeful revenants,
Everyone paid to this new acquaintance.
Space where there wasn't appeared from nowhere
Like this small universe was expanding out of thin air
A gasp of wonder, an impenetrable barrier envelopes him.
Nobody dare touch this new member, so different within.
The new guest's clothes, haircut and skin
Was the same, the latest fashion, what was currently in.
The new member of the gathering just shone bright.
But there was one thing different, like a beacon of light.
For all those around to stop and politely stare,
This new arrival only needed to be in his wheelchair.

Allegic to Stairs

The Bandersnear

In days come, entertained, and gone,
It was the thing everything came to fear,
This apex predator dominated the food chain,
Nothing was safe from the bandersnear.

Prowling ancient lands for simple meals,
Eyeing neanderthals with an evil leer,
As big as a bear but lightning quick,
Nothing escaped the bandersnear.

Never sleeping, always alert to chances,
Pouncing on an unprotected rear,
Everything a target for its rapid attack,
Nothing can predict for the bandersnear.

Moving from place to place without effort,
The lightest footsteps no being can hear,
It moves like a ninja without all the drama,
Surprise was key to the bandersnear.

The deadly highwayman shuns all company,
Nearly every second of the year,
Except when the situation is perfect,
A rarely seen moment to the bandersnear.

Two of the earth's most fearsome beings,
Meet and spread panic so severe,
They multiply in the heartbeat of danger,
The terrifying birthday of the bandersnear.

The population has grown to the present day,
Its stealth is making numbers unclear,
Adapting to the city with great ease,
Watch for the attack of the bandersnear.

Matt Gopsill

It can happen to you in the day or at night,
Making you scream or shed a tear,
This creature is fear in the personified form,
You will never escape the bandersnear.

The Eruption

Red light on the pitch black horizon,
Glowing like the fires of hell,
Clouds billowing like rough waves,
Emitting that rotten-egg smell.

On the peak of the tallest mountain,
Casting a permanent shadow down,
The opened gateway to the underworld shines,
Ash floats over in a deathly gown.

Gone is the snowy white peak,
Evaporating to scalding steam,
Replaced with a vicious spray of lava,
Straight out of the darkest dream.

The island's sacrifices didn't please them,
Dying in their unholy names,
Valiant village elders specifically chosen,
But pointlessly frying in the hot flames.

The mountain tribe felt every shudder,
Each rock-fall leaving its dent,
Trees and bushes uncontrollably burning.
Even their main totem pole was bent.

Tall fountains of magma lit up the night,
Spraying boulders all around,
Rain started to collect all the deadly ash,
Making it into new fertile ground.

Then the terrified tribe heard a roar,
Coming from the mountaintop,
They saw something truly strange:
A massive demon with a huge mop.

In a booming voice like cannon-fire,
It said in an apologetic tone,
"Satan has got a major leak in his en suite,
I'm the plumber he had to phone."

Then in the joint blink of the tribe's eye,
The demon had fixed the damage,
He stopped the damned leaky volcano,
Then he told them to waste-manage.

"I had to clean out a blockage in there,
The volcano was full of people all blooded,
Use the ground provided for your waste,
We don't want Satan's toilet all flooded."

The Final Meeting

"Good afternoon, Sir; how are you today?"
Said the hooded figure beside me,
I noticed he was very tall in my confusion,
I replied, "I'm as well as I can be."

I looked around, seeing the fog
Descend around us like a net curtain,
Shadows passed like fish in a muddy pond,
Details of the world becoming uncertain.

The hazily photographed image appeared,
A car embracing a shocked tree,
The airbag bleeding from the steering wheel,
But in the middle of this carnage was me.

I couldn't comprehend the scene I saw,
The ultimate out-of-body experience,
The shadow-like figure spoke,
"You never get used to the gory violence."

It continued to talk in a deeply cold voice,
"You had a pretty decent Mercedes there.
Shame about the patch of hidden black ice,
Sometimes life and death isn't fair."

I looked at the origin of the talking,
A face hidden inside a jet black hoodie,
Above some darker Nike tracksuit bottoms.
He just said, "Get with the times, buddy."

I replied to this tall stranger looming,
"I thought you carried around a scythe."
"It's in for sharpening," Death boomed solemnly,
"I have a hire strimmer," he said with a writhe.

I began to get over the shock of the moment,
And curiosity overtook my fear,
"Do you know where I'm going to?" I questioned,
"Or will I be haunting drivers right here?"

"I only do the point of death,
I never go into the afterlife department,
I haven't got the relevant paperwork issued,
They don't let me in that compartment.

"I'm just the meet and greet for your transition,
A friendly face to help you on your way,
I had a holiday in the late eighteen hundreds,
And I'm still clearing the ghosts today.

"I think your ride's about to arrive on the left,
I hope I've been helpful with your passing,
Please mind your step into your Lamborghini,
I have backlogs of ghosts amassing."

With that my final meeting ended with a roar,
As my ride appeared from nowhere,
I turned to wave to my black clothed greeter,
But I couldn't see the hoodie anywhere.

The super-car door opened wide,
I stepped into the nice new car smell,
One last look at my lifeless earthly body,
Thank God the car said heaven not hell.

The First Bloom

A red point of colour shining amongst the grey stones,
Rubble scattered randomly across the land's bare bones,
Twisted metal tossed aside like autumn leaves in the wind,
Dead tree trunks cowering away from where they were pinned,
Their leafy green life blown away like an extinguished candle,
Gone is that token of love carved in their its bark by vandals,
In their place, a wood of metal pylons in tortured shapes,
The centre filled with a power plant's corpse where a hole gapes,
Its blood and energy exploding over this monochromatic wasteland,
A lifeless scene of devastation poisoned by particles fanned,
By manmade winds of a harsh winter spread for miles around,
Radiation dosages deadly to all living on this ravaged ground,
Ash as deep as fresh snow covering like a duvet,
Blocking the tenacious sun rays and keeping spring at bay,
But enough restorative light squeezes through to the land,
Invigorating a seed to grow a poppy in the sand.

Matt Gopsill

The Harbour

The conversational clinking of yachts in the harbour,
The running commentary of current affairs,
Ropes and dreams blowing in the sea breeze,
Water waving away your cares.

Spinnakers fluttering despite their bound restraints,
Hinting at their unbridled colours,
Gleaming hulls flying their forest of flagpoles,
Trying everything to outshine the others.

The melodic beat against stone as the tide enters,
Its regular visits bring nutrients to wildlife,
Always politely knocking and waving as it comes,
Familiar greeting like a kiss from a wife.

A shrill alarm calls from overhead,
The ultimate scavengers on constant watch,
Discarded chips, crusts and cornetto cones count,
As their favourites to swoop in and catch.

An archetypal cry bounces around,
Echoing off the sea-worn harbour walls,
Selling today's catch at sale prices now,
Drawing customers with their loud calls.

The bustling activity in an aging hub,
The harbour lazily wanders through time,
Lagging behind its commuter population
Attracted by its famously low rates of crime.

With the best sea air money can buy,
A piece of history on your own doorstep,
The right move just for you on the market place,

Allegic to Stairs

A must-have for any high flying sales rep.

With the modern world getting away from it all,
On the unchecked cobblestone roads,
Under the rust-covered cranes waiting for a haul,
Standing patiently for their long gone loads.

The ingrained smell of seafront toil
Wafts out of each aged flagstone,
Trodden in by generations of fishermen,
Their trade taking years to hone.

Sitting in the middle of this timeless vista,
The seafront line invasion of the new,
The harbour where the old comes to dock,
Sit with an iced tea and enjoy the view.

Matt Gopsill

The Night It Happened

This is no ordinary poem,
Filled with flowers and enchanting woods.
This is a tale of horror,
Filled with the obligatory virgin's blood.

On a dark and stormy night,
The nights where only these acts occur,
The innocent, happy-go-lucky Jessica,
Went on a walk fuelled on cherry liquor.

Nobody saw her leave her house,
With trimmed bushes and picket fence.
Strolling on the road to nowhere.
Phone and cares left indoors without any sense.

Jessica was floating on a cloud of alcohol,
She hardly made a splash in the waterfalls.
She didn't notice the crows flying around,
Oblivious to their shrill warning-calls.

Her mind was full of beautiful music,
Lyrics about fairies and a magical life.
The darkness was packed of intrigue and wonder,
Memories of her childhood were rife.

A figure was lurking in total darkness.
Ready to take Jessica by surprise.
This night wasn't quite so innocent,
This was the night that "it" would arise.

The rain bounced off his bald head,
Streaming into his bloodshot eyes.
Dressed in a heavy leather jacket
All adding to the black, menacing guise.

Allegic to Stairs

He slinked stealthily towards her,
With hell's thoughts burning in his mind.
'This innocent teenager will be easy,
Just right for the rack I've designed.'

Quick as a hungry cobra he pounced,
Knocking poor Jessica to the sodden floor.
Her delicate skin cruelly pierced through,
Liquid enters like a dream opening a door.

Fuzzy light slithered through a crack in a blind,
Reality came knocking like a mad-man.
Broken glass and half eaten chicken wings,
Strewn around this mouldy caravan.

Tightly bound with fraying duct tape
To the specially-made rust-covered rack.
The leather-covered bald man before her
Stepped up and gave her a smack.

Just then something happened inside her,
Something she hadn't felt before.
Her muscles and tendons were growing,
And she gave out an almighty roar.

Jessica's teeth were like razor blades,
Sharpened to an inch of their lives.
And her freshly manicured nails
Resembling a fine set of knives.

The bald man stood there before her,
He felt as tiny as a little shrew,
The virgin's blood gushed over everything,
As the organs and bone shards flew.

Matt Gopsill

His eyes were fixed on the victim,
Tearing her way out of her blouse,
The final blow cut off his bald head,
And Jessica strolled back to her house.

The Political Poltergeist

Don't call me a poltergeist if you please,
I don't mess or push anything like most,
I love everything tidy and in its own place,
Also never ever call me a common ghost.

I am a ghost with the height of decorum,
Manners fit for the Queen's banquets,
I roam the corridors of the utmost power,
My placement is as good as it gets.

My last workplace was a total nightmare,
A student flat in Leicester's Highfields,
I couldn't rest in a bit of peace,
Constantly tidying the smelly minefields.

Yes I know I'm no ordinary poltergeist,
I have never thrown a vase off a table,
I love my domain clean and in order,
I'd hold everything in place if I was able.

I float about the house on Downing Street,
Passing politicians and dignitaries daily,
Listening to private conversations with ease,
Watching over priceless ornaments gaily.

But lately things have turned for the worst,
Members of parliament coming and going,
Place names on the mahogany table changing,
Rumours and gossip flowing.

Brexit, Brexit, every damn day,
Faces contorted with pressure passing,
In a rush to get to the latest crisis meeting,
All this hatred and blame amassing.

Matt Gopsill

Nobody stopping to admire the lights,
On our festive Christmas tree,
Or the unique gifts from around the world,
All of them brought so thoughtfully.

I even had to catch an old Chinese vase,
That blundering oaf knocked on his way,
It was from the Ming dynasty and simply perfection,
Its lasted longer than him, unbroken to this day.

Straightening rugs and wiping fingerprints,
These new cabinet members don't care,
More interested with their phones nowadays,
I need things to be tidy, it's not fair!

Going in and out with mud on their shoes,
No time to wipe their soles it seems,
Dragging in dirt and germs to their work,
I'm afraid this place no longer gleams.

I have put in a transfer request today,
I'm fed up with the work and stress,
I want to go back to the student house,
Number 10 is in too much of a mess.

The Trolls

There are trolls at the bottom of my garden,
They are there to stay,
Hidden among the rhododendron flowers,
Living their secret way.

Well manicured lawns and tidy flower beds,
On a prime acre of land,
Every perfectly placed pansy growing just so,
Every inch meticulously planned.

Each bright-green leaf at the start of spring,
To the gallery of autumn,
All the twists and turns of the garden path,
Planned down to each ripe plum.

But at the end of this leafy paradise,
A wicker fence hides the beasts,
Under the neatly pruned bushes,
These unsightly trolls feast.

Dining on fruit and bright flowers,
The bounty of my perfect garden,
Spoiling the brilliance of this backyard,
Putting it under great burden.

Pulling up the freshly mown grass,
Plucking the vibrant petals,
Leaving bent teeth-marks in the plums,
Even clearing space for nettles.

The vista of cultivated beauty they spoil,
This garden paradise lost,
Daisies in the grass and paving going crazy,
Even the salad gets tossed.

But from the broken ground, wild plants grow,
All the colours of the rainbow,
Complementing the cultured foliage design,
And together new seeds are sown.

This naturally beautiful and bountiful plot,
Supports trolls and owner alike,
Precisely balanced in colour and purpose,
Time flowing endlessly; dreamlike.

This eden has a very unique sign post,
With the perfect garden boldly named,
This green and most pleasant land,
'The name of life' it proudly exclaims.

The Two Trees

Rock-solid heart wood,
Sturdy fountains of tangled roots,
The two giant redwoods stand together,
A stable, ever-growing pair of brutes.

King and Queen of the windswept forest,
Rotting leaves and branches surround,
Dappled sunlight struggling through the canopy,
Hitting the damp, life-giving ground.

Two colossuses together -
Seeds once missed in the mists of time
Now dominating this gnarled ancient forest,
Rulers of the kingdom in which they climb.

Hundreds of creatures around them,
Living in dark and gloomy holes,
Overshadowed by the two's majestic beauty,
Protected by these immense wooden poles.

 Climbing their way out of the darkness,
Their tangled leaves yearning for light,
These two amazing redwoods,
Public yet private - what a sight.

The Unforgettable Poem

Thoughts of rhyme and reason fill my head,
Like passing ships in the dead of night,
The memory fades leaving a trail of waves,
I can't remember, try as hard as I might.

The ultimate nighttime barrage of creativity,
Happening behind my closed eyes,
My brain awake writing beautiful words,
With no way of release til sunrise.

The unforgettable poem forming in my brain,
Perfect prose and punctuation produced,
It was safely tucked up in my memory banks,
Stored for tomorrow to come from its roost.

The poem relaxing on a fluffy bed of neurons,
Gathering its thoughts for the big reveal,
But it had a chance to have a lie in,
Now it's gone to where memories congeal.

It should have been out in public and shining,
Filling the world's airwaves with its beauty,
Being read out by hundreds of adoring people,
Endlessly giving pleasure and doing its duty.

It could have been published in magazines,
Seen by the most eminent poets around,
Picked up by the press and spread worldwide,
Becoming several countries' national sound.

Instead its artistic verses died,
Before they could spread a lyrical wing,
The world will never know its beautiful lines,
The unforgettable poem no-one will sing.

The Valley Walls

A deep valley in a rugged land,
The river bursting with rain,
Surrounded by the audience of autumn,
Trooping the colours of November pain.

Light poured in like the thick army coffee,
Drunk in trenches a hundred years before,
Bouncing off leaves of every shade of orange,
Some dying on the wet floor.

Vibrancy surrounded the rough river,
Flecked with the golden brown fallen,
Discarded in their final flourishes of life,
There husks floating by all swollen.

Waterfalls of raindrops forged downwards,
Gathering together like armed battalions,
Parting the valley's ancient stony defences,
White light sinking like galleons.

Five concrete walls carve this valley up,
Man-made borders controlling the flow,
Building up pressure and tension behind,
Commanding lives on when they can go.

Five front lines of immense hostilities,
High speed projectiles go bursting out,
The deepest roar of deafening impacts,
But you can discern an individual shout.

Darkness invades this huge rocky trench,
Vailing the vibrant community within,
Life hunkering down against the winter,
Muffling its wild lifetime din.

Matt Gopsill

The battle of life and death goes on now,
A century after the so-called end,
We remember each valuable life given up,
Sacrifices we all struggle to comprehend.

Unseen Interiors

They didn't notice him at first,
Even though he sat right there,
Conversations flowed round him,
Sound waves rushed by unaware.

Like a mossy stone in a choppy river,
Part of the scenery but often overlooked,
An obstacle to avoid or peep underneath,
But never disturbed or allowed to obstruct.

His solid exterior was hard to break,
The interior unseen by many,
Shiny gemstones or precious metal lie,
Hiding qualities worth quite the penny.

Gazes avoiding these rocks in the river
Of people's hands waving front and back,
Life rushing like water over these individuals,
Dripping in the little hole in their rain mack.

These bedrocks of society are important,
Rolling around with jobs and many skills,
Hiding in all their unseen interiors,
Are treasures that help scale life's hills.

Interiors of wisdom and determination,
Degrees and experiences as well,
Disabled people may be hard to see inside,
But they have some great stories to tell.

Matt Gopsill

Who Wants to

Who wants to walk on their own two feet,
Striding about the city, six feet tall,
When that uneven pavement waits for you,
To give you that very nasty fall.

Who wants to use their own two hands,
Creating new works of art,
Only to see them superseded by others,
In the ever-changing tastes of the heart.

Who wants to talk with their own mouths,
Struggling to be heard in the many voices,
Saying the wrong thing in the vital moment,
Ruefully backtracking your word choices.

Who wants to see with their own two eyes,
Watching the horrors of this insane world?
Making new nightmares for you to experience,
Sweating in the night as your dreams swirl.

Who wants to hear with their own two ears
To the bullies pulling you down?
Destroying your confidence and self-belief,
Until you're just the class-clown.

Who wants to feel with their own heart?
This fragile but sustaining organ beats,
Parading it on their sleeve for some people,
In the deadly game of passion it competes.

Who wants to live the picture-perfect life,
Without sorrow or the pain of loss?
No nightmares of this imperfect world
No wild rivers to swim across.

Allegic to Stairs

Who wants a lonely meaningless existence,
Drifting for days on a flat and tranquil sea?
No problems to overcome to show your skills
Who wants a boring life like that? Not me!

About Matt

My name is Matt, and I am just a normal man with some wheels strapped to me. My background is in computing, which I thought was where my talents lay, but in my spare time I write poetry.

At first it was just to get things off my chest (and, yes, sometimes for Valentine's Day). I soon found that I really enjoyed writing and people loved what I had written, so I semi-secretly wrote more.

A few years ago I went to The Word open-mic night with someone who was performing. I really enjoyed listening to the different genres, and decided to ask if I could read one of my poems. Rob Gee was the host, and we knew each other, so he said 'of course'. I was a little nervous because I use a computer to talk for me, and I had never spoken a poem out loud. But the performance went okay, and I got a round of applause! I had to tell everyone I was writing poetry then!

My writing has come on so much from then in quality and quantity - writing poetry about any topic, be it funny or serious. I just wait for inspiration to come; I never know what poetry I am going to write next, which is the exciting part of it. I have now set up a blog called partdalek.com and I am always looking for an open mic night or a poetry slam to compete in. I hope you enjoy my first book!

SanRoo Publishing

To find out more about SanRoo Publishing visit our website at:

www.sanroopublishing.co.uk

Follow us on Facebook @acalltowrite

or on Twitter @SanRooriters

SanRoo Publishing
is part of
Inspiring You C.I.C.

26 Bramble Way, Leicester, LE3 2GY
Registered Company No. : 1021381

www.ingramcontent.com/pod-product-compliance
Lightning Source LLC
Chambersburg PA
CBHW070439010526
44118CB00014B/2107